Hit the Street

✠ ✠ ✠ ✠

poems by
Hank P. Lowinger

Hit the Street

CONTENTS

Beauty Beyond (1963)

she starts to smile
says the whole world's passing on by her
once in a while
what was real is now denied her
nowhere to go but fast
will it last
will the right one come and see her

lost in her dreams
like the pieces of a puzzle
helpless she seems
never knowing her endless struggle

nowhere the flowers bloom
is it true
would the right one come along and be true

but she never saw the writing on the wall
never knowing why she had to stand so tall
why did everyone want her but not at all

she starts to laugh
with her thoughts so deep embedded
not knowing soon
her own world would soon be ended

and pass alone
blue eyes and blonde
beauty beyond

but she never saw the writing on the wall

Been Up to the County

been up to the county late last week
found me a place beside a creek
gotta get down the land
gotta lend a helping hand
can't let yourself be down,
only get one time around
been in a hole with a sorry stained soul
been better off than dead like the people said
go out and get to the land
go out and lend a helping hand
don't let yourself be down, you only get one time around
been to see the preacher man
he said boy do the best you can
gotta get down to the land

Black Girl (1969)

black girl smiling at a party
brown eyes forever to be
she held my hand and whispered
lay your body down next to me
should I follow my instincts
go on up to her room
I found the sweetness
cow jumped over the moon

Dad

I loved him as a stranger
I never knew him well
all the times we spent together
seem real enough for me

we never seemed to notice
that time was slipping by
a brief glimpse of love surrounded
but who knows who, where or why
I really do miss him
I expect him to come through the door
I flash on his reality
but reality is never more

I sense my own mortality
my children I hold dear
I wonder if he felt the same way
with death ever so near

he was just a taxi driver
he gave me the gift of life
I love him and I miss him
I fear for my own life

Death Row (2001)

I'm just sitting here on death row
got plenty of time on my hands and I got nowhere to go
20 more minutes are left in my life
I'm gonna fry for killing that bastard who slept with my wife

you can sit there and judge me right or wrong
aren't you supposed to rehabilitate me?
18 more minutes, then I will meet my destiny

so can you write a letter to the governor of Tennessee
and ask him to grant me clemency
I'm just watching the red phone on the wall
hoping that soon he will call

capital punishment they say it's the answer to
that, you got to take an eye for an eye
8 more minutes, then I know I'm going to die

the seconds they are going by so fast
meal in front of me will be my last

cheeseburger, french fries and Coca-Cola
nothing fancy left for me
1 more minute
then I will meet Mr. Eternity

but that's how things are going to be
I know that I can't change history

I just want to be free

20,000 volts of electricity

Dead Man Walking

dead man walking on the sky
asks no questions
tells no lies
see you in the by and by
I'm just a dead man walking
on the sky

I'm the one who loved you
so when you are sad

I am the one you can embrace
I am the one who you can chase
no one can replace
your dead man walking
on the sky

Down to Your Soul (1992)

I met her on a Tuesday
hair it was flying
her eyes they were blazing
her heart it was true

I knew right away
I really did love her
she was from among
the chosen few

sometimes I wonder how we stayed together
through all of our lives' tribulations
people who see us, they don't talk softly
black and white ain't the world they want

when I tested HIV positive
I thought for sure
you'd run away

but you stood by me
like a tree to the forest
you stood by my side
to my last dying day

you saw me coming
walked on by my side
held my hand tightly
didn't take my love lightly
you saw me coming
and showed me you loved me
love in your heart down to your soul

Dream of Impossible Happenings

on a soft cloud I'm passing, my baby's gone
she stayed so true to my name
over stars that are shining, my spirit slept
our love it grew just the same
do you remember the feelings past?
they touched your soul beneath

oh my love is a feeling I can't explain
so true an exception
so blue are my feelings gone
so true in rejection
do you remember the things in our past
far out, they touched my very soul

so let me go, let me go down the highway
I will understand
how it is that you looked at me sideways
I could never plan
all the others, they do it their own way
they cannot understand
how it is I got to do it the right way
I am the "man"

but my eyes looked real deep
at my personal sins, like sleep
it was a dream of impossible happenings

The Drug Addict (2013)

I woke up in the gutter
my life was in shambles
all of the things that I wanted to be
trying hard to figure out what really mattered

I know I'm not coming home
left you there by yourself alone
you're out on your own

sometimes you just
got to look in the mirror
and see the things you don't want to see

I know I done you wrong
lied and cheated from the start
just broke your heart

wel, I sit in this prison
four walls all around me
trying to think of the right words to say
how much I love you, how much I miss you
going to love you forever, forever a day

so please can I have
one more chance

can you find that small space in your heart
we can make a new start

a drug addict's story is never over
because the end is just the beginning
of finding their truth as they go along their way

trying hard to figure out what really matters
it's the love in their heart
another day being drug-free

Echoes

echoes of my past beside me
guide me each and every day
echoes of my past remind me
the falling ways to stay
the noise within my head is starting
I can hear it every day
other times it tries my patience
tranquility shows the way
life, it holds many obstacles
I built a road to find the way
that leads me to acceptance
future love is here to stay
beautiful life it's daily order
touch the hand for another day
let me know that you love me
I will love you anyway

End of the Day

in the morning when I wake up
all the time we were together
all the things I took for granted
all the things I let get away
nobody else really matters
all my love seed I've scattered
I want to hold you in my arms

I know you're the one
left me there, gone and had some
fun and yes
came home to stay
I want to hold you in my arms
at the end of the day

End of Love

why did it happen to me
how was I to see
that things would end
you walked out the door
said you were no more
in love with me
I just want to die
sit down and cry

it's not hard to see
but it was meant to be
it is the end of love
nobody knows
how to close
the wounds of love

all the people say
I'm going to have my way
and find my own true love

Everyday

see them stare
say I care
If I dare
learn to share

hide the key
let me be
If I see
what's for free

on a roll
make my goal
takes its toll
dig a hole

see the light
have to fight
make it right
loves tonight

I can see
you're the one for me
everyday

Everyone's Felt That Way

have you ever had one of those days
when nothing seemed to go right?
when the world seemed like a maze
and everything was dark as night?

if you ever felt like that
then you know what I'm talking about
everybody's felt that way
and I feel that way tonight

did you ever feel alone
wondering just why it was so?
looking for a better place
and not knowing where to go?

did you ever search the night
hoping you'd see a shooting star?
when suddenly you felt the fright
of not knowing who you are?

The Fool (2001)

I'm the guy with all the answers, considered a ladies' man in
my day
but nothing could have prepared me for the minute when
she looked my way

It's the kind of stuff you see in the movies
of a love that is destined to be

in my heart there was no other, wow gosh did I love her

it was plain to see, she's the one for me
destiny, electricity

so we decided to live together, even talked about family
but I couldn't make the commitment, wanted her and still be
free

then one day she simply vanished
disappeared into thin air

all the things that mattered
somehow I just shattered
it's a shame
I'm the one to blame

now all I do is look for her
I go here there and everywhere
just to tell her how much I love her
how much I really care

in my heart there is no other
boy, did I love her
it's plain to see
she's the one for me
like electricity, it was destiny

sometimes you gotta look in the mirror
see a white horse or a mule
you've got to face the truth now
you're a fool

Freedom (2001)

a word that has meant much to me
people will die for
people will cry for
just to live in the land of the free

free to go on out now and seek your own fortune
let no man persuade you and all men agree
and in the end you can write your own true story
of the glory of living in the land of the free

I grew up on main street in downtown Toledo
I thought life would be easy as pie
drafted in sixty-four, fought in the Vietnam War
watched as all around me, my friends they died

so I sighted them down in my sniper scope
pulled the trigger on their humanity
and all the killing I was doing
so that you could live in the land of the free

so I came back to the USA
I thought things would go my way
but the people just spit on me

they were against the war
said, "what are you killing for?"

I'm killing so you can be free
free to go out and seek your own fortune
where no man persuades you
and all men behave and in the end
this is my own true story of the glory
of killing for the land of the brave

Friend Unto Me

I saw him last week
he looked the same as before
I still see his face
smiling back from the door
well I waved with my hand
I cried in my heart
never once did I think
that we'd ever part

many times we had traveled
down the same troubled road
by having each other
helped to lighten the load
there were so many changes
that both of us shared
and so little we wanted
much less for we cared

he's a friend unto me
I'm a friend unto him
and we both gotta laugh
at the places we'd been

Gang Boy

grew up in the big city
place where they take no pity
left there out on his own, alone

no sisters or brothers
not like the others
his father never did bother
to give him a name

joined the bloods at fourteen
drive-by shootings, the scene
did five in juvenile
learned to read after a while

all of the others
just like his blood brothers
all felt the same
who's to blame?

Haunted

haunted by memories of his being
I can't escape the pain
I lay alone at night
as dark as fallen rain

I reach out and want to touch his face
he seems so close to me
to be held so warm in his embrace
his love my destiny

often in my heart I feel
that no one understands
the love so special
beyond real

as I wander through this life
thinking of what's to be
what I just really want to want
Is to meet in eternity.

Heart Broken Flowers

I look to the future
I hold my head high
of the things I have wanted
many have gone, or many did fly

go out and find her
tell her the truth
your love is here to stay

you're there to remind her
you're not aloof
from feelings of love every day

I'm like the heartbroken flowers
who can't find their way

If I Promise

If I promise
just to love you
will you marry me?
If I promise
just to hold you
will you finally set me free?
all the others, they don't matter to me
in your heart
you just want to be free

In Love with a Stranger

I fell in love with a stranger
felt secure in her arms
I couldn't see the danger
overcome by her charms

so go on out and find your way
and let the truth be known
there's so much that I want to say
it's the time, it's the time for you to come back

people they all look strangely at me
my shame I cannot hide
that's the way things turned out to be
who is really on my side

I know I cannot change the past
make things the way they should be
please just give me one more chance
to make our love last

I know I lost my way
couldn't find it on my own
I just want one more time to say
it's the time, it's the time, to come back home

everyone has their times of shame
the truth is hard to see
it's easy to move the blame
look deep inside for what it can be

Killing Time (2002)

well he's killing time, trying hard to find
all the things that always stay on his mind
things that he wanted to be
and places he wanted to see

so he climbed the highest mountain and he reached up and
tried to touch the sky
to find the answers in his heart, to find the reasons why
life is short and he did know that everyone must come and
go

well he sits in front of his TV and gets his dose of tranquility
watching all the things he's told, the things he needs as he
grows old

so if you are one of the lucky ones that somehow just stays
on the run,
it is clear to see you really are a lot like me
life is short and life is sweet
he found a way to be discrete

well his life was this happy one
full of love and all kinds of fun
and all the places he wanted to see and all the things he
wanted to be

so he climbed the highest mountain and reached up and he
could touch the sky
surprised to find just like the birds, he spread his wings and
he could fly
his life was short, his life was sweet,
he found a way to be discrete

while killing time,
time slips away,
we're all killing time.

Killing Youth (2002)

everybody's looking for answers
to the problems in our own society
all the deaths and senseless killings
seem to multiply
I'm just sitting here wondering why

well, you read it in your newspapers
watch it on your tv's
all the senseless killing of our young
all the experts say
it will soon go away
I fear the worst is yet to come

so go on out and seek your fortunes
don't follow a crazy path to fame
revenge and retribution
really ain't a solution
truth is we are really all the same

mothers and fathers, sisters and brothers
trying hard to explain
all the unrequited violence
followed by death's silence
is killing each other just a game?
what a shame

Last Song, Sad Song (1989)

if you see me out on the corner
all decked out in my hoodie
thinking money is the answer
fast money the thing I want
I ended up on the wrong end of the day

I have traveled around the country
seen the people their happy faces
thinking they have all the answers
money walks and talks
it takes them places

I am simply seeking
the true answers
knowing that life is just the chances
we take every day

this is my last song
it's just like a riddle
I'm just the monkey
caught in the middle
of the search to find peace and true love
the fact we cannot rise above
because black is white

wrong is right
up is down
my head just spins around

it's my last song that I'm singing
to my true love, so far away

Life in the Streets

life in the streets, you are
on your own every day
up and down the avenues
never knowing which way
all your possessions on your back
is it really better this way?
life in the streets, you are
homeless, at home to stay

Lonely

how I would often like to be
one of the sun's yellow bursts
one of the lucky beautiful things
that radiate
but I am of a quiet breed
one of the carefree careless lonely
smiling to hide the gloom
that penetrates
and who among the chosen people
would care, would dare to step from
a sun-filled room
into
that is mine?

Long Road

lovely day on the long road
that takes me back to you
can you feel your heart
Can we can make a new start
it's a long road I want to travel

Looking Out My Window

looking out my window
strange things are happening outside
looking out my window
I just want to run and hide

whips are crackling and rustling
strange things going on outside
I'll just stay here at my window
I'm not getting in line

faces at my window
pass long in time
man calls up to my window
says buddy come get here in line

I'm not getting in line
I'm not fighting no war
no no, not me anymore
no...

Love Lost, Lost Love (2001)

in recognition of Eugene Lazar/Bobi

he grew up in NYC
bricks and buildings tumbled down
fell in love with the girl so pretty
their lives turned upside down

what is it that really matters?
is everything and nothing the same?
I run like the "mad hatter,"
looking for who is to blame

how do I ever recover
from the lies I know are true?
everything around me reminds me of you

died in the arms of strangers
how could this be?
all the love they wanted
they'll never see
it's love lost
lost love

Love's Blind

sometimes I feel so happy
other times I feel so blue
happiness all around me
especially when I'm thinking of you

if you see me on the streets of Brooklyn
walking around with my heart in my hand
tell me now how you still love me
tell me now how you still understand

I remember how she would hold me
so tight I thought I would die
her legs wrapped around my shoulders
love so deep, it made me cry

this is not the end of my story
I still hold her love in its glory
I still hold her hand in mine
love so deep, hearts intertwined

cause love's blind
love's kind
love's blue
love's true
love's here
love's everywhere

Love is the Answer (1998)

do you remember, along the way
back in September, you came to stay
your hair was braided
you were looking good that day
you smiled and told me
your love was on the way

I saw her standing
out by my way
her eyes were smiling
couldn't think of words to say
so I walked right up to her
said hey! what's up today?
she smiled and told me
her love was on the way

will she still love me
along the way
sure as the heavens above me
her love is here to stay
she's cleared my spirit
she lets me be me
loves me to the limit
she sets my soul free

love is the answer
each and every day
you too can find the one you love
along the way

Master Plan (1994)

this is the story of my good old friend,
he was a man among men,
he stood so tall

who are we to judge him, was he right or wrong
he always got along
he always sang the right song

then he met his favorite girl
her hair was all in curls
her eyes blazed her love for him
then she became his woman

he got the virus, and he did die
reached up and touched the sky
he would not let us cry
for then, did he understand
he is part of the master plan
for all to be

My Friend (1986)

I had a friend
he lived his life in a beautiful way
loved and lived
life to the limit
never looked back
enjoyed the day
he showed me the way

always took the time
just to listen
loved the family
every day

he got sick
HIV virus
that's serious
it cost him his life
but he never gave up
he fought and he struggled
with every ounce of his strength he fought
to live on and on

who, who, who knows the future
who says that they know it all
step up here and take your best shot right at it
step up here, can you stand up as tall
step up and show me the way

My Love

her hair was fair
her eyes were blue
she only looked my way
I held her hand
I touched her heart
her love was mine that day

I know that soon we've got to go
but yet to find our way
somewhere in my heart I know
our love is here to stay

so many times, my past has led me
down the road to stray
but this time it feels so right
to take it day by day

if you see me coming
please move to the side
please don't get in my way
life's too short
life's too sweet
It soon will be my day

Need a Friend

I met her when I was only 21
thought life was about going out, getting high, and having fun
but I didn't know the score
seems more of the time I watched her
as she went right out the door

now it is time to be free
do those things in my life, just about me
then I'll go and see the setting sun
all my life's about material and getting things done

sometimes I wonder if I'm going under
things they always seem the same
people and places, all of the faces
just want to play a game

if you want to hold me
tight in your arms and never let me go
I think you really want to scold me
keep in your heart, the things you cannot show

now I turned 51
seems my life's about going out, getting high, and having fun
I can't even begin to keep the score
seems the women in my life are like a revolving door

but if I grow up, perhaps I'll show up
and no longer will pretend
that I'll soon discover, the perfect lover
who will love me till the end, she'll be my friend

Nelson Mandela

he was a fella
who somehow
overcame great adversity

people who hate
soon learn their fate
like all the others
they beg for mercy

No Words Can Explain My Love (2010)

no words can explain,
no words no cries,
no words can explain
no words no cry
no words no cries
no words can explain, my love

I'm ready for the world
I've found true love
body to body
the peaceful times

everyone wants the chance
to find their love
eyes open wide
lay down side by side

look out I'm back
my love's on track
I know I've grown
I'm coming home

everybody wants the chance
to find true love
body to body
the peaceful times

Not at War

I am not at war with anyone
so take back all your bombs and planes
all they do is bring hurt and pain

send my love to the Iraqis and the Americans
send my love the Israelis and the Palestinians
because war itself is really hell
and dead men got no tales to tell

revenge and retributions will
how many more people do you got to kill?

why is violence the only way?
can't we find a way for peace today?

when can we finally disarm
killing can only do harm

we've got to find a way to talk
you know, dead men cannot really walk
I am not at war with anyone

all parents want their children alive
give them a chance to live and thrive
I am not at war with anyone

Now

so I look to the sky
flying so high
wondering why
who is worthy

of the life we all seek
the strong and the meek
end up in the same place in history
Now

Odeed

met her on a Monday
my heart stood still
met her on a Tuesday afternoon
I met her on the corner, oh what a thrill
why'd she go?
I loved her so

I held her hand
my heart stood still
held her hand in the afternoon
held her hand, oh what a thrill
why'd she go?
I loved her so

she asked to love her
my heart stood still
she asked to love her soon
she asked to love her, oh what a thrill
why'd she go
I love her so

will it last forever?
I know that it will
hope eternal tells me so

lasting moments, united until
we got to go
I loved her so

she died on a Monday
my heart stood still
odeed in the afternoon
who can explain it?
would have to know
I loved her so

Ordinary, Extraordinary Man (2018)

shadows are falling, nighttime is near
people are calling, for the things they want to hear
while all of us others, we just go on our merry way
it's the time to remember
ordinary man came by that day

I met him when he was a full grown man
those of us who knew him well
understood he had a plan
to help all the others, who like he stumbled on their way
it's the time to remember
ordinary man would have his way

if you saw him coming
you had better move aside
many tried hard to avoid
but all of them then cried
out for their long lost lovers who had left and went on their
way
it's the time to remember, ordinary man had come to play

he has left this Earth, against his will
many said he moved too fast, but he was standing
still helping all the others, who like he fell on the way
it's time to remember, ordinary man did fly away

nighttime has fallen, the sun has disappeared
people are holding close the things they want so now
while all of us others
we just skip along our merry way, it's the time to remember
ordinary man, extraordinary man did pass away

Once in a Dream

my thoughts are like a story
my mind fills all the glory
my heart fills the nakedness that comes with
passing time

singing songs of wonderment
the opposite, its complement
the treasure of its happiness
is hidden deep inside my mind

fantasies and prophecies
the still unanswered mysteries
or clear defined hypocrisies
will be answered in the far unknown

life is one sensation
that came with hesitation
that left the complication
of self-imposed ideologies

books are written regularly
of man's defined humanity
it's the abyss of seeming thoughtfulness
that is seen and overcome by hidden lies

love's deceit—reality
the truth beneath sincerity
felt between the feeling consciousness
that occupies the joy-filled ride
where there is no place to hide

beauty's beast, it's the obvious
it's the image of your own self-repulsiveness
it's the eyes of societies' meaninglessness
that defines escape's frivolities

the interposed reality
the sense of sterility
the unheard voice called "stability"
separates the so-called "man" from all mankind

my story's got no ending
like life itself, it's bending
toward the void called "time," it's pending
toward the fate defined, "so near to be"
it's the same fate for you and me

Places in Heaven

people cry
want to die
have to buy
don't know why
everyday

get high
get by
reason why
have to lie
every way

see the sky
wonder why
have to die

people show
they got to go
want to know
every day
they get their way

take a stand
make a play
hold my hand
to the promised land

Prison Blues

(Bad news is my middle name)

I once thought bad news was a letter
thought that it came in the mail
now I know I was mistaken
bad news is my middle name
bad news is my middle name

it started when I was a young boy
it all ended when I was a man
this story is not a sad one
I dealt the cards I played the
game hard
bad news is my middle name
bad news is my middle name

searches, chains, they took me away
behind the great walls they put me to stay
if bad news is your middle name
well take my advice, stay out of the game
bad news is my middle name

Questions of Love

I met a girl
her eyes were bright
she held my hand
stayed the night
feelings true I could not hide
love will last? who can decide?

feelings hidden in her heart
how do I know her dreams?
I never want to part
why is love never as it seems?

is she forever, can it be?
openness is on our side
together, somehow we do share
our love's forever, everywhere

love is her mystery
will she ever set me free?

Remember Diallo, Dorismond (2001)

the people of plenty
usually get their own way
most of us others are soon forgotten

one time or another
we all gotta play
police and garbage on the street
smells rotten

meet me on the corner of your mind
you're not forsaken
all God's children once were strangers

sometime or another
we all look the other way
police on the corner represent danger

why is violence
their only answer?
can't we find a better way?
good friends should not be forgotten

hope, it springs eternal
your very last day

the future is in your hands
you gotta find the way

good people should not be forgotten

Shattered Dreams (1999)

we all want to know why
we were born, raised, live and die
we have expectations riding high
we have time to laugh
time to cry
I will see you in the by & by
lay me down my grave
with a sigh
I just ran the race
could not fly

when you see me on the street
you know my heart skips a beat
I will smile at you in my defeat
let you know you are not my sweet
come and go with me
and be discrete
lay me down beside your body's heat
I just ran the race
ended in defeat

shattered dreams your destiny
shattered dreams were meant to be
you and me
you and me

The Soldier

in recognition of Dr. Peter Pinto

he was only six years old
when his mother left him in the cold
out on the streets of Baltimore
prostitutes were coming right through the door
so his aunt came down from Buffalo
twenty-six degrees below zero
back with her on the greyhound bus he went
and he grew up there so tall and strong
trying to figure out what was right or wrong
he only wanted to be
just ordinary like you and me
and in the end he wanted to know
how does time come and go?
so he joined the marines in sixty-four
the Vietnam war was on our shore
A.I.T. sniper man, he became part of the killing plan
so he killed and killed, killed and killed
never seemed to lose the thrill
bodies, they piled up to the sky
and then he found he could not sleep
he was counting bodies instead of sheep
so they shipped him back to the U.S.A.
Staten Island hospital, V.A.
shot him full of Thorazine
post traumatic stress was the theme

so he climbed the walls and hit the road
to sunny Californ-i-a
he went up coast to Eugene, Oregon
on a commune farm he worked the land
he finally lent a helping hand
his love with mother nature proved a charm
then he met her on a rainy day
her hair was blue, her eyes were grey
she held him in her arms so tight,
he finally could sleep through the night
somewhere in the great somewhere
he found someone to really care
and in the end he could finally see
he was ordinary like you and me
and in the end he would finally know
that time will come and time will go
and in the end we all will know
our time will come, our time will go

Stuck in the Middle

she was just seventeen
her heart was on her sleeve
she simply adored him
his love she could believe

they stayed together for the next 10 years
their lives became so different
it only led to tears
the love they held so dearly
it somehow disappeared

they were stuck in the middle
solving the riddle
of their lives

Sweet Lorraine (1972)

met her at a party
her name was Lorraine
we stared at each other
my life would never be the same

she was an aspiring actress
I was on my way to fame
was it a sexual attraction?
who knows who was to blame

she said let's split this part
I said let's go to bed
she said she simply adored me
couldn't get her out of my head

was it wrong to love a black girl?
ebony and ivory
in a world of segregation
would our love ever be?

why did it happen?
who can explain?
was it simply a romance?
her name was Lorraine
sweet Lorraine

Thinking of You

all of the others
were just like my mothers'
way of loving, while holding you afar
oh how I miss you, long so to kiss you
it's true, I can't stop thinking about you

when you told me you no longer loved me
and your heart turned to stone,
I couldn't take it no more
walked right out the door
went to live out in the world out on my own
so I wandered the city
slept in the alleys
looking for love in a bottle of beer
oh how I missed you, longed so to kiss you
it's true, I can't stop thinking about you

how do others reconcile their differences?
and get their love back on track
I still love you like heaven above you
I want you in my arms please take me back
so I stand in the shadows beneath your window
watching you in the arms of another man
oh how I miss you, long so to kiss you
it's true, I can't stop thinking about you

Time Flies

you seize the moment
can you see it pass by?
time's flying
we never know why

can you hold on to time?
look up and see the sky
the clouds are passing
boy, can time fly

seek out the future
the future is now
time is flying
someday, somehow
I see time flying

Tomorrow

I'm going to the highway in the sky
flying high
without a sigh
tomorrow

people all wonder why
they have to die
without a cry
tomorrow

I'm in a bind
going out of my mind
how I wish I could find
tomorrow

if you knew the incident
from where I went
you'd consent to
tomorrow

let me take your hardened heart
away from the land
return you to the sand
tomorrow

sing our songs
carrying on
you can come along
tomorrow

True Love is Hard to Find

people, places, their bright shiny faces
true love, it finally came my way
and in the end, she was my friend
my broken heart did mend

I met her on the corner
I knew she was the one for me
and if I try
I know I can fly
why did mama tell me boys don't cry?

true love, it is so hard to find
close your eyes, she gives you peace of mind
in her arms you know you're the only one
the only one

Twenty-One

I reached out for the heavy fun
but, that's life at twenty-one
more things, but it was just none
can't keep the time as before

if you come, let me know when
things are changed
I can't forget
all the good times
they seem to go

I can't see forever
I must not slow down

Very Last Beat of Your Heart

trespassers will be prosecuted
to the fullest extent of the law
signs like this we read every day
love, it's gone away

people who see us walking
hand in hand in the park
black and white, they don't know wrong from right
love, it ain't in their heart

sometimes I sit and wonder
jut how lucky I am
to have the chance, just to find true romance
love, it has come to my heart

people will come from all over
to hear the words of the man
still, I will know
that we are all going to go
back to the earth and the sand

so hold me close
squeeze me tight in your arms
promise me still
you're going to love me until
the very last beat of your heart

Walk On By My Side (2001)

I met her on a Tuesday
her hair was flying
her eyes they were blazing
her heart it was true

I knew right away
I really did love her
she was from among
the chosen few

If you see me coming
just walk on by my side
hold my hand tightly
don't take my love lightly
if you see me coming
just tell me you love me
love in your heart, down to your soul

sometimes I wonder how we stayed together
thru all of life's tribulations
people who see us, they don't talk softly
black and white ain't the world they want
when I just tested HIV positive
I thought for sure

you'd run away
but you stood by me
like a tree to the forest
you stood by my side
to my last dying day

Want to Know

want to know, have to go
steal the show, get a blow
job every day

have to move, in a groove
not so smooth, lots to prove
in a day

hold her hand, take a stand
be a man, share your plan
anyway

in the park, have a lark
be a spark, after dark
go on your way

will it be, can I see
is it me, who'll be free
in this life

eat a scone, stand alone
by the phone, never moan
every day

drive the car, never far
to a bar, you're a star
in your mind

ride the bus, love's a must
things are just, filled with lust
for your girl

We're All in the Game

in your life you find a friend
and everyone believes that life won't end
truth be known
we are alone
can't put off what we postpone
love's the same
who's to blame?
we're all in the game

What the Years Do

hold my hand, let me go right
show me the way through the night
let her heart go to you
see what's right, just you two
have some time to be true
and the years go bye
how many times you think of her
just love her

Who's Gonna Pray for Timothy McVeigh?

everybody is looking for
the answer that would open the door
to why things changed on that fateful day

bombs went off and lives were lost
human suffering was the cost
who's gonna pay for Timothy McVeigh?

celebrated the fourth of July in Oneida county
fought in the desert storm war,
he knew what America was fighting for

he and Terry McMillan
decided they would do some killing
drove the bomb truck to the building
in Oklahoma City on that fateful day

they strapped him to the gurney
injected the lethal solution
families of the victims believe that they
have gained their absolution

capital punishment, they say
gonna stop murder today
the truth be known

our greatest terrorist was homegrown

his mother and father still
gonna spread his ashes on bunker hill
who's gonna pray for Timothy McVeigh?

Wonder Why

people cry and wonder why
how come it is they can't touch the sky
life, it just seems that way
and in the end, you'll need a friend
and somehow we all do tend
to love the wrong one on our way
people sigh and wonder why
how come it is they have to die
seeking their truth along their way
in your heart, you had to part
and find someone new to start
the cycles that lead astray

You Grew Apart (2002)

when you are all alone
just sitting by your telephone
waiting for your man to call
is he the best one of them all?

and if he's the one you're waiting for
he'll soon be knocking on your door
a smile will broaden on your face
you know no one can take his place

and why every time, did the sun refuse to shine?
he held you in his arms and told you you're
forever in his mind

you spent all those years with him
raising up your kids
you never got close enough
to know exactly what he did

time has passed you by
you're getting on in years right now
never knowing what love was
wondering why where who or how

and why did you and he
drift so very far apart?
is love supposed to be forever
in your open heart?
changes subtle as can be
you knew them from the start

how many times you wander
through your only life
never knowing what love is
thinking that you were alike

and if you could change things
what exactly could you do?
would you go on forever
never really being you?

and if you look deep inside yourself
you will finally see
a person, place, time and space
you never thought you'd be
and in the end you knew
deep inside your open heart
you grew apart

Hank P. Lowinger was born in NYC. He received his master's degree from Hunter School of Social Work and worked his entire adult life helping people. His poems are reflections of his experience as a clinical supervisor for adults and youth with substance use disorders. He currently lives in Rego Park, Queens with his wife.

www.ingramcontent.com/pod-product-compliance
Lightning Source LLC
Chambersburg PA
CBHW021020160726
47994CB00006B/2590